Notably Quotable:
Words to Ponder

Author: Troy Shaw

Notably Quotable:
Words to Ponder

ISBN: **978-0-9983245-5-5**
Copyright © April 2021
By Holam Books & Media
First Edition

Notably Quotable:
Words to Ponder

Author: Troy Shaw

ACKNOWLEDGEMENTS

I am more than appreciative for my proofreaders.

DEDICATION

I dedicate this book to the God of Abraham, Isaac, Jacob, my father, and my father's father. With love, this book is dedicated to my mother a woman full of witty words for the world.

PREFACE

Words are alive, as we may never speak them without breath
– may the words hereafter live to help, heal, and inspire hope.

Notably Quotable:
Words to Ponder

Author: Troy Shaw

"If you cut the blood supply a tick will fall off"

"We need a relationship with God whereby we stop letting other people interrupt God in our lives!"

1

"Cursed money is worth less than black market food stamps"

"Games create winners and losers-so play to win"

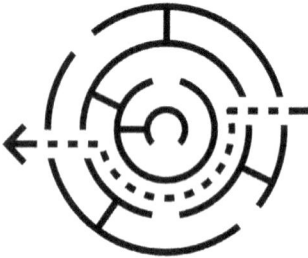

"Doctors may remove a bullet, but venomous words may linger forever, what you say can be worse than an assassin's bullet"

"Be careful dancing in the garden, snakes may be hiding in the grass."

"They say if you take one step God will take two, I say if you take one step, God will step more than you can count."

"The Devil would love to see us all burn, but from the cross Jesus took us from cremation to celebration."

"If you want to check your DNA – If you want to know if you are connected to God, if you want to know if you are truly connected, check your heart. If your heart bleeds love then you are in there, if you can love your enemy, love those that hurt you, if you know how to forgive and love despite the world's hatred then you are in the family."

"We need hope as an active ingredient for faith which requires us to materialize the desire to please God, the substance of things hoped for"

"You couldn't win a bowling tournament wearing football cleats – sometime the proper equipment is essential. Winning souls for the Kingdom isn't done while wearing hatred."

"Oh, "when did we" was the answer. The hour of fear and trembling before God in need of Christ resembling. The sheep from the goat was the way the Shepherd seeks the pure the light of judgement in that day. Will you be ready with your work all done? The least and lost await your service God the Father, Son and Spirit have already won."

"Read your Bible, God can do anything – create man, deliver humanity from the flood, set ice on fire, part the Red Sea, tame lions, turn water into wine, feed multitudes and He raised Jesus from the dead. Read your Bible it's all in there – nothing is too hard for God."

"The pain of surgery is sometimes necessary for healing."

"There are campaigns across the country to end distracted driving. It's dangerous to everyone around, it puts your life in jeopardy. Distracted driving is an uneducated practice that proves a lack of intelligence. Nevertheless, I wish someone would launch a movement to end distracted worship! It puts your life in danger, hinders your connection with God, possibly distracts others, and it's demonic to personally reduce God in your life."

"Don't be so quick to judge, like a boomerang your careless thoughts will return. All you can afford to throw is marshmallows when you live in a glass house and all of us live in the weakest structures of reality often feeling protected by false fleeting foundations fortified by fantasy. You're not protected any more than the next human, all of our righteousness is but filth.""

"If you hold your neighbor's feet to the fire long enough, your feet will get hot-what goes around comes around!"

"Because of Jesus there is no mystery-the veil has been torn, the curtain has come down, the covers are off and all of us have personal unlimited access to God, love covers a multitude of sins."

love

"People are struggling across the globe, yet we cannot let the number of global issues discourage us, suppress us, or stop us from working toward change – change mercy, justice, morality, kindness, and lingering love. We must speak truth to power, get the word out as a watchman on the wall-sound the alarm for righteousness.

"You cannot lock an open door."

"Never kill the cow for meat if you need milk."

"If faith were a tree it would produce works."

"God can draw light from darkness - the Crucifixion of Christ is the ray of light in the Valley of the Shadow of Death."

"True prosperity comes when we learn to praise God for what we have as opposed to pestering God for what we don't have."

"The first Passover was before the Exodus." –

"The rains from a storm can bring destruction and life to the same field. We must trust God to feed us from the results."

"The more we magnify God, the more we see God as God is"

"Anytime you choose without God you've made the wrong choice, void of wisdom and future."

"They say beauty is in the eye of the beholder, we should be glad that God looks at us through Jesus"

"God will make you so happy as if you'd turned yellow and smiled like an emoji."

"We all sin, but thankfully not all at the same time, love your neighbor as yourself."

"Never try to reduce the power of God, thinking that God can't change your neighbors - don't forget you live in the neighborhood. Give grace, you'll need it in return ."

"Facts will need faith at times, but faith will never need facts - God can do anything."

"We should want to be with Jesus, simply because we love Jesus – not because we would rather be with Jesus than live in Hell."

"Always laugh with God and not at God"

"Remember when the forecast of your emotions called for extreme precipitation on your face. Tears rolled down like showers from a thunderstorm, the winds blew across your tears and you felt the cool just to know how sad you were but then Jesus spoke words of peace and your storm became joy."

"We should feel grateful, not entitled – God has blessed us with so much. Gratefulness says we're humble, while entitlement makes us arrogant"

17

"The Bible is the best selling book of all times, many people own a Bible – but actions prove that few read it."

"We must learn to see the many blessings that God has bestowed upon us. Far too often, we suppress blessings while magnifying our sadness, lack, and deficiency – when we would be exponentially better if we embraced God on the brighter side of life ."

"If you walk a mile in my shoes, keep them – I've got a new pair and moved on."

"I'm here to tell you that we should never count God out. Never disregard God. In narrow escapes and last minute situations, God still has plenty of time. God's ways, God's time, and God's thoughts are not our ways, time or thoughts-God's ways are always beyond superior to any solution we can ever come up with. God can when nobody else can."

"A democracy of fools is a failing government."

"GPS doesn't need to know where I started to give directions from where I am, it sure would be nice if people were like that."

"My grandmother used to say, "if you lie about one thing, you'll lie about another." In hindsight, her words were practically prophetic. Lies are so overrated these days-the truth is the only way out of a prison of lies"

"Faith without works is dead and works without faith are weak."

"Self-righteousness can render us stupid, we see their mess and think that's what we smell, when in fact if we just look down – we're standing in our own. You never have to look away to find a sinner, never have to leave home to find a mess, even a deserted island would become polluted upon your arrival."

"Parents should limit punishing and grounding children, don't punish them for life-never make your children feel that redemption is unachievable. When redemption is erased, perpetual punishment will either break the individual or the individual will break the system. God provides us with correction not condemnation-redemption flows from the love of God not retribution. I'm so glad that God's redemptive grace issues another chance."

"When life is disconnected
Time is drenched with sadness
Despair dances with the day
Dancing like a dervish of doom

Setbacks saturate the journey
Trials, temptations, secret snares
Bothered, betrayed, and bent

Wait on God, with faithful heart
Wait on God through strain and struggle
Wait on God – never forget the comeback at Calvary.
Wait on love and be encouraged forevermore."

"When the ship sinks it is time to move on beyond the
vessel that once carried you, life jackets are less stable, but
greatly appreciated when that is all you have-our ship
often sinks to bring us prospective."

"No coach has called for his kicker on first and goal-have
faith in your opportunities."

"Pig wrestling is dirty business, don't get in the pen unless
you planned to get muddy. Resist acting like the ungodly
– it's dirty business."

"Any road leads away from God, only one leads to God – Jesus is the only way."

"Patiently wait on the last minute before your breakthrough and the first minute will be forgotten."

"Listen to the game before you learn to play and you might get good."

"If you're mad and God is blessing you, nothing changes if God takes from you and gives to others - you should be fine, nothing changed, you're still mad."

"Steam will cease once the water cools and the water will cool once the fire goes out – the steam may distract you, nevertheless the fire is the problem."

"Humanity fit optimums, cum hoc fiat millirem."

"You couldn't win a bowling tournament wearing football cleats – sometime the proper equipment is essential. Winning souls for the Kingdom isn't done while wearing hatred."

"We have to keep working together through our differences. Even teeth and tongue clash at times, nevertheless they should never stop working together-life depends on it."

"Jesus is preferred to take away our sins. You can try Rinso, Borax, or Bleach-you can soak sin, scrub sin, or rinse sin and the stain of death will remain. Sin will seep deep into our hearts never to be removed by human strength, ingenuity, or science-Jesus alone, Jesus alone."

"If it looks and smells spoiled, don't taste it - because it probably is spoiled."

"God has ignited you with the purifying presence of the Holy Spirit and there is great discomfort in attempting to maintain God's presence while remaining spiritually out of place, the burning power of the Holy Spirit will simulate pain within the crucible of correction causing our hearts to burn from the precise laser of divine change."

"You can shoot a bear, but gnats are nearly impossible to scope."

"If Caucasians think its always okay for them to play Jesus in the movies, then they should give Africans the opportunity to play Caesar, Einstein, Pope John Paul II, and Ronald Reagan - IJS."

"Our community needs after school programs and economic development, we need civil action, and social justice. Our community needs leaders that will speak truth to power. We need to care for the single parents, the sick, sad, busted, disgusted, low, leveled, least, and lost. What would Jesus do? We are called to teach and baptize-not condemn and criticize."

"We think we're so supreme with the ability to launch missiles on each other when the invisible brings us to our knees."

"While your busy trying to see what I look like, God sees who I am. God sees who you are, God sees us hears us, and cares for us far beyond what we look like. God loves us beyond our flaws, God also sees beneath."

"The amount of water determines your status-drinking or drowning. Moderate boundaries make sense."

"A drop of toilet water can ruin a whole glass of the best wine."

"Think about it, you've seen the results of power, but you've never seen power, it works behind the scenes. Are you powerful?."

"Who can fight the invisible?"

"If someone says you're the apple of their eyes, then you should find out if they like apples."

"You may never be better than you could be, but you can always be better than you are."

"We should consider our resources, far too often we're planning to cross the ocean before realizing our community lacks a road to the shore. We must start where we are to manifest where we want to go."

"Darkness alone has never extinguished even the tiniest flicker of light – so boldly shine no matter how dark the night may become."

"When the time comes, clocks will not matter."

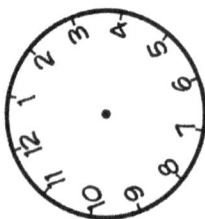

"How will you spend your last days? Jesus, Moses, and Peter used there last days to remind us of God's great love and our mandated commitment to the precious love of God? We must live like Christ, loving the world to the very end. Christ gave his life, God sacrificed God for humanity. Would you die for this world?

Would you die for drug addicts, would you die for rapist and sex offenders? Would you die for convicts, muggers, murderers, and liars? Would you die for your worst enemy? Would you die for a pimp, a child molester, or a drug pusher?

Would you die for the least, lost, and last? Who would you die for? Would you die for the dirty, disgusting, and dangerous? Would you die for the drunk driver, would you die for the one that owes you money, lied on you, or cheated you? Would you die for him, would you die for her, would you die for me? Well Christ did and we must follow..."

"I love you beyond those three words and ride or die with you beyond those three – where two or three are together there is power, a three strand chord is stronger than two."

"The photographer may remember the race, but will never win it."

"Don't let a trip to church cost you your soul – come to receive and leave to serve."

"It's still dark before the break of day."

"Busy is good, we have a better chance in a flood over a drought."

"It may take a lifetime to find a opportunity, too bad some of us destroy it in less than a minute."

"Don't give up, until time is up – a close finish is still a win."

"Beware of a free lunch, you may await slaughter once fattened."

"You may rest assured when family and so called friends are invited – enemies are automatically included."

"Black people have never been what American propaganda declares us to be, just as America has never been great for Black people - from 1492 to the present an apology, fact or otherwise has not been issued. Even empty word has been found too valuable to utter from the lips of earthly privilege.

If America is the greatest country on the globe - then Black people have nowhere to go. We await Christ return, our great hope. Blood calls Black people to vote, our people lost their lives for us to exercise citizenship - nevertheless blood calls us to Christ, as God sacrificed for us. The blood calls us to the action of love and truth.

When we answer the call of the blood we vote as we must live, with the consciousness of Christ forever guiding us. America is not great and never has been. I pray that someday it will become great, as it learns to forgive as Black people have for the 401 years since our ancestors were tragically kidnapped. I pray that it will become great, because after all my people-built America without compensation. The greatest challenge for us is to reject becoming bitter, while embracing the better way of Jesus.

America has yet to show me greatness, it has displayed greed, corruption, enslavement, oppression, and evil. Yet I believe that we can always hope for change. Nonetheless, I am persuaded that God's love will see us through. No matter the outcome my aim is higher ground because I know that God is great - always has been and always will be great."

"The miraculous unfolds from God's power once man and nature step aside to watch the Lord work."

"Crazy how life keeps you stressed trying to live while racing to die as we kill ourselves, whelp lol – happy thoughts."

"Stems linger long after flower blossoms fade."

"Learn from music, let your notes be heard, live in the spaces, and enjoy the rest."

"Never look a gorilla in the face
– it may attack."

"The grass is still growing while you mow it – progress is not always permanent."

"Sometime the grass is much browner on the other side."
"We live on purpose when we rearrange our thinking from today to a day to."

"Uber and Doordash can't deliver like God delivers."

"Six feet apart is better than six feet under,"

"At what point does a virus gone pandemic become negligent homicide?" #investigate

"Roaches are survivors, perfectly designed to run and hide – how do you survive and what are you designed for? #Love"

"Just as football can't be intelligibly played without a football, the Christian life cannot be lived without Christ. Just as no ball or a golf ball could not substitute for a 🏈 football - nothing and nobody could ever pinch-hit for Jesus."

"It's hard to keep the lights on if you don't pay the electric bill."

"Most ghettos have mice and roaches, that hide and run for shelter, skeptically managing their environment. Adverse surroundings often require people to do the same."

"When you focus on what you lack on not on what you got, soon what you got will be that which you lack."

"Following Christ will require that we take up the cross and follow the Messiah - as Calvary is an unavoidable destination, we know that the crucible of pain produces the joy of resurrection glowing with the arch of Christ return. Advent lifts the expectation of hope as love, peace, and joy shine forth from the depth of every dark night - joy to the world! "

"If we win the fight against temptation in the snack aisle at the grocery store – we will have no struggle at home."

"If food is your medicine, then your backyard can be your pharmacy – God has provided us with the earth and the fullness thereof."

"When you share the outhouse, you don't get to choose the flies."

"We can see and understand many sides but only 1 matters – LOVE"

"It's easier to stand on the ruins than to rebuild the city – grandstanders pose while builders work."

"A suicide bomber is not the victim – falling on your own sword does not make you a hero."

"Donkeys and elephants are both circus animals – don't emulate caged sideshows."

"The tunnel will never be completely dark as long as there's a light at the end."

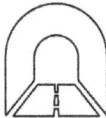

41

" Benjamin Franklin once said, "don't make yourself a sheep, the wolves will eat you." I'll tell you people are either sheep or wolves - one is cared for and the other must hunt to eat. It's best to be a sheep when the Lord is the Shepherd - there is always more than enough in God's green pastures and protection extends beyond the valley."

"I once witnessed the slaughter of a hog – the entrails articulated the echo, you are what you eat."

"True faith breeds forgiveness – it's when you look beyond problem and person to see God."

"Success and progress end the same."

"Every hour is an opportunity for failure or greatness."

"Be thankful for closed doors, sometimes it's better to be locked out than locked in."

"When attempting to build a bridge, one must have resources on both sides or risk constructing a diving board."

"Words like please may gracefully lead or follow a statement as a the people that use them track and trace life with expectation."

"Counterclockwise corrections must be made counterclockwise and never in reverse."

Keep moving forward, pressing toward the mark set by Christ.

HOLAM BOOKS & MEDIA

Holam (חוֹלָם) is a Hebrew niqqud vowel sign represented by a dot above the upper left corner of the consonant letter. For example, here the holam appears after the letter mem (מ): מֹ. In Modern Hebrew it indicates the close-mid back rounded vowel, and is transliterated as an "o".

www.ingramcontent.com/pod-product-compliance
Lightning Source LLC
Chambersburg PA
CBHW071935020426
42331CB00010B/2887